I0158292

Croquet

Rules of the Game and Official Laws

By the British Croquet Association

PANTIANOS
CLASSICS

Published by Pantianos Classics

ISBN-13: 978-1-78987-549-2

First published in 1920

Contents

Plan of Croquet Court

For dimensions see "The Court." See also Rule 40.

4

Croquet and Its Rules

Croquet is a comparatively modern game. It has not the weight of years on its side to increase love and regard for it.

The name seems to indicate France as its origin, and it is said to have been brought from there to Ireland, thence to England.

Public match games were played in England as long ago as 1867. As a lawn game it became exceedingly popular, and the formation of the "All England Croquet Club" was succeeded by several annual contests for championship at Wimbledon.

It has been even growing in favor of late years in England, judging from the formation of clubs and the public contests in different parts of the country, schedules of which are carefully published at the beginning of each season, thus eliciting a widespread and increasing interest in the game.

Leading Features of Croquet

One of the strong points about Croquet is the ease with which the game can be established. Almost every home in village or country has some grass plot large enough and level enough for a goodly place to set out the game. One can readily see that no elaboration is needed. Mark the boundaries by a strong white cotton cord, drive the stakes and set the arches with some little regard for precision (See cut opposite) and the ground is ready. The lawn should, of course, be closely shaven and rolled, and to prevent the grass from disappearing utterly in certain places where progress is most difficult and the wear consequently the greater, each setting out of the game may be in a different place.

As a test for good temper, forbearance and fairness no other game, we believe, to be superior to Croquet. It is the little amenities of life that count largely in any system of play or business. These add a flavor and produce results along character lines. To win is sometimes the crowning ambition. But with it frequently goes a lack of modesty and an increasing regard for self that destroys the possibilities of development of finer things. It does not require the handling of immense sums of money or the entrance upon large business enterprises to find out the good qualities or the opposite of your associates. And we may be pardoned from our long experience in connection with Croquet (sometimes in closest competition for national honors, more frequently, however, with the friendly tilt, keen and close, between rival experts) if we drop this word of caution to beginners. Let every movement be one of fairness and honor. Let your adherence to the rules be observed in all cases of even the greatest interest. Let not self-interest mount so high as to warp your judgment and let the little acts of comity and courtesy be sprinkled in between even the most difficult plays, so as to realize outside of and away from what any expertness may bring, the richer fruits of pleasant, though rivaling, companionship.

We have known characters vastly improve by courteous companionship and prevailing geniality on the Croquet ground. The old-fashioned wordy strifes and contentions, cherishing and continuing ill feeling, are now unknown and aside from any beneficial physical advantages these features must also be regarded in taking stock of the benefits of Croquet.

There is in the game of Croquet a great opportunity for displaying one's ability, judgment, nerve, coolness and boldness of play. A valuable discipline comes to the eye in connection with the movements of the hand. But the game of Croquet is peculiar.

In a game like base ball, or lawn tennis, mere quickness is sometimes the great desideratum. But the deliberation that can be manifested in Croquet has hardly a parallel in the entire round of athletic sports.

Good Instruction Needed

At the very beginning there should be selected and secured, if possible, some good instructor and player *combined* (not every good player is a good instructor) so that the tyro may start right. *"Well begun is half done."* The correct position, the proper methods or lines of play, the nice points of the rules; all these should, if possible, be *taught by some suitable person* so that progress may be more rapid and results all along the line be more satisfactory. We would like to re-emphasize this point in the matter of instruction. It is absolutely essential. Every kindred game and every study in any branch of learning and science point *to the necessity of excellent instruction at the very outset.*

Position in Striking

Many different positions are assumed by wielders of the mallet. The so-called "pendulum stroke," made with two hands — the mallet swinging vertically between the legs well outstretched — has grown in favor much the last few years. As one commences so he is apt to continue. There is much reason in using the pendulum stroke. It is philosophical and as near being mathematically correct as possible. But its gracefulness is questioned, and ladies are practically debarred from its use. There is also a one-handed stroke — made vertically — sometimes between the legs and sometimes outside of both. But the stroke is made in each position with the eye of the player directly over and in line with the desired movement of the mallet.

Principal Points in Playing

The common experience of our most expert players points to the following as the chief points of excellence in play that should be aimed at even in the beginning of one's participation in this pleasant mode of physical exercise:

First. — Striking a ball so as to make it hit another, be the distance great or small. This will be a matter of *acquisition* on the part of most people. We have known the poorest hitters to develop by patient practice and perseverance into great ones. No progress can be made in the game unless one can make one ball hit another. The eye must be accurate, but both the eye and the hand need to be trained. The same accuracy is needed in the making of arches from any distance.

Second. — Ability to cause a ball to go a certain distance, just so far and no further, e. g.:

(a) To make it take position near to another ball.

(b) To give it a position in front of its arch.

 (c) To wire it (if the danger ball) so that it can have no direct shot on a ball.

(d) To put a ball beyond the open shot of a ball already wired.

Third. — Ability to drive the object ball to any desired position

To do this successfully requires the manifestation of the greatest skill. It wins games. To hit a ball full means driving it straight ahead, when force and fullness of stroke are desired, the former depending upon distance desired. Then, to make a ball pass to the right or to the left requires it to be struck in a certain way on account of angle or direction desired.

Fourth — Closely allied is the so-called "*Jump Shot*" (see page 65), i.e., making your own ball pass over another ball or over one or more arches, causing it to hit another, otherwise impossible to be "*captured.*"

The Wickets, or Arches

For beginners narrow arches would destroy interest and discourage effort. At the start the arches should be at least 4 inches, and these can be replaced by more difficult ones as expertness in play increases. The wire should be at least one half inch in thickness, and to secure firmness should be driven into the ground at least ten inches, leaving tops about ten inches high. If blocks should be used it would mean, of course, greater fixedness. If tops are square they can be driven more readily into the earth. If no blocks are used changes in setting out the game are easily made, as the lawn becomes worn in some places by excessive use.

The Balls

The balls may be of wood, but those of hard rubber are the most satisfactory. Though costing much more at the outset. they are cheapest in the end.

The ordinary game for Tom, Dick and Harry will find a well-made wooden ball to be in keeping with their expertness, and later on, as general play increases in excellence, a better ball can be secured.

The Stakes

The stakes may be of any hard wood, about one and one-quarter inches in diameter set at the middle of the court just outside of the playing line and projecting above the court only an inch and a half, so as to allow a ball to be shot from in front of it in any direction.

The Mallets

Here is opportunity for the display of taste and expenditure as well. At the beginning the mallets found in our ordinary equipment will be found to answer all purposes. The price list, however, shows varying qualities of excellence, and the expert player will always have his own mallet, his favorite, as a billiardist has his own cue, and so he takes it with him and deems it a decidedly individual asset, very rarely lending his own, and as rarely using the mallet of another player. These mallets are of great variety as to length of handle, length of head, diameter, weight, kind of wood, metal bands for protection, etc, etc.

One end should be equipped with soft rubber, as this feature allows certain well-known shots or strokes to be performed with ease, which otherwise would be quite impossible.

Colors

The rules are made with reference to the four colors, red, white, blue and black. The first three are easily kept in mind as to their order, as they are the order as used in speaking of our national colors-the "Red, White and Blue." If the balls have not at time of purchase these colors they can easily be kept in fine coloring with little labor and expense. This is so desirable that we give here minute directions for painting balls. First, drive three 2-inch nails into each of four pieces of inch board, about four inches square, so that the projecting points will afford, when the blocks are upturned, a place to put the balls while being painted. Buy an ounce of Chinese vermillion, one ounce of ultramarine or Prussian blue, one ounce of lampblack and four ounces of flake white, and one-half pint of ordinary shellac dissolved in alcohol. Take four old saucers, one for each color, and get four small varnish brushes. For white, red and black place a little of each color singly in a saucer and pour on it some of the shellac, mixing it with brush till it is thin and uniform; then paint the balls on their supports and they will dry very quickly. For a fine blue color place in a saucer some blue powder and with it some of the flake white, as the blue itself would be far too dark if not tempered with white. A little experience will give one fine colorings. Only a little powder is needed each time. The brushes must be kept in alcohol or water when not in use. If rubber balls are used no black color need be obtained, as the ball is black already.

The Clips, or Markers

These will come with the equipment but will need painting occasionally in accordance with Rule 5, i. e., painted on one side *in full* and on the other *in half*. The manner and rules for affixing are also given in Rule 5.

The Court

Any level lawn with grass closely cropped, which has a length of sixty feet and a breadth of thirty, will answer for a Croquet court. A court even twenty-five feet by fifty has been known to furnish great chance for pleasure and exercise. The court may be large or small, according to desire or amount of space to be had, but a court with larger dimensions than these first mentioned is not advisable.

The simplest form is the rectangular with a good strong cotton twine for boundary limitations fastened by four substantial corner staples (see Rule 40). With the rectangular form, on a court 30 x 60 feet, the arrangement of the arches or wickets and Stakes may be as in the diagram opposite page 41. The size of court is optional. Each stake is set just outside the playing line half way between the end corners, the first arch eight feet from the boundary line and the second seven feet from the first— the side arches in line across the field with the second arch, and five feet nine inches from the boundary line.

The Center

The center arch may be single or double, and may be called also the cage or the basket. If double, the arches should be placed at right angles to all other arches and 18 inches apart, so that the ball in making the center arch will move in a direction across the field, instead of in the direction of its length, as with the others.

The grounds, however, may be laid out in various ways. The Prospect Park (Brooklyn) Croquet Club, has a very peculiar form of court which any club, of course, is free to adopt.

We have known grounds also to be elliptical in form. But while each club in many respects *may be* a law to itself, there is, nevertheless, much benefit to be derived from a uniform plan of doing things.

In the placing of the arches there is also an opportunity for considerable variation. Our English cousins, who of late have given a great deal of attention to Croquet, place their arches widely different from the method employed in the United States, where uniformity generally prevails. This game is one in which we should much like to see an international uniformity, if possible, as a basis for possible international competition for honors in this attractive outdoor pastime.

[Note. The publishers are pleased to state that the English Rules have been constantly before our Supervising Editor, and wherever advantage could be gained in points or phraseology, he has felt free to make use of the same.]

Terms Used In Croquet, With Their Definitions

Ball in hand. — A ball that has roqueted another ball.

Ball in play. — After a ball in *hand* has taken Croquet it is a ball in *play*.

Bisque. — An extra stroke allowed at any time during a game.

Bombard. — To drive one ball by Croquet so as to displace another.

Boundary line. — The outside limits of the court.

Carom. — A rebounding of a ball from stake, arch, or another ball.

Combination. — The using of two or more balls to effect some particular play.

Croquet. — To place one ball against another and play from it or with it any way. This is imperative after a roquet.

Danger ball. — That ball of the adversary which is to be played next — "the guilty ball."

Dead ball. — A ball from which or upon which the player has taken his turn since making a point It is then *dead* to all direct shots till he makes another point, or has another turn or play.

Direct shot. — When the ball struck with the mallet passes *directly* to another ball, or makes carom thereon from a stake or an arch.

Drive shot. — A shot made so as to send the object ball to some desired position.

Finesse. — To play a ball where it will be of least use to adversary.

Follow shot. — When the playing ball in taking Croquet is made to *follow* the object ball in nearly or quite the same direction.

Foul strike. — A false one — one at variance with the rules. See Rules 7, 11, 16, 20, 31, 33, 44.

Innocent ball. — The last played ball of adversary.

Jump shot. — Striking a ball so as to make it jump over any obstacle between it and the object aimed at.

Limits of the cage. — See Rule 53, and illustration opposite p. 64.

Live ball. — A ball upon which the playing ball has a right to play.

Object ball. — The ball at which the player aims.

Odds. — Extra stroke or strokes allowed by superior players to equalize playing. (See Bisque.)

Playing line. — Line real or imaginary 30 inches inside of boundary line on which balls are placed for *playing* when they have passed beyond it or outside the boundary line.

Run. — The making of a number of points in one turn of play.

Scoring. — See Rule 6.

Shot, or Stroke. — These have the same meaning.

Split shot. — Any Croquet from a ball upon which a ball has counted.

Set up. — A position of advantage secured by a player in the interests of his partner ball.

Wiring. — To wire a ball is to place it so that it will be behind a wire (or arch), thus preventing an open or direct shot.

Croquet Rules

[Note. — The following rules are adapted to the playing of *Loose Croquet*. — A few notes will be found at the end after the rules.]

INTERFERING WITH PLAYERS

RULE I.

No player, or other person, shall be permitted to interfere with the result of a game by any word or act calculated to embarrass the player, nor shall any one, except a partner, speak to a player while in the act of making a stroke. (See note to Rule I, p. 63.)

ORDER OF COLORS

RULE 2

The order of colors shall be red, white, blue, black, but the game may be opened by playing any color.

MALLETS

RULE 3

There shall be no restriction as to kind or size of mallet used. One or two hands may be used in striking. For different strokes mallets may be changed as often as desired.

RULE 4

Should a ball, or mallet, or stake, or arch break in striking, the player may demand another stroke, with another ball or another mallet, and stake or arch properly placed.

CLIPS OR MARKERS

RULE 5

Every player shall be provided with a clip or marker of the same color as his ball, painted in full on one side and on the other side only the upper half, which he must affix to his arch next in order in course of play, before the *partner* ball is played, with the full painted side toward the front of the arch. Should he fail to do so his clip must be placed upon the arch upon which it was last placed and he must make the points again. Should he move his marker back of the point he is for, attention must be called to such error before the *partner* ball is played, otherwise it shall stand. Should a marker be moved beyond the proper point, it shall be replaced, provided attention is called to the error before the point upon which it rests is made. Should a player put a ball through its arch, he must move the corresponding clip to its proper arch before the next ball in order is played, otherwise the clip remains as before. No player shall lose any point or points by the misplacing of his clip by his adversary.

OPENING OF GAME-SCORING

RULE 6.

All games shall be opened by scoring from an imaginary line running through the middle wicket across the field, each player playing two balls of any color toward the boundary line at the head of the court. The player, the center of whose ball rests nearest this border line, shall have choice of first play and of balls, provided that, in scoring, the ball did not strike the boundary line, any other ball, or the stake. The balls shall then be placed on the four corners of the playing court; partner balls diagonally opposite to each other, the playing ball and next in sequence to be placed on the upper corners, the choice of corners resting with the playing ball and all balls being in play.

BALLS-HOW STRUCK

RULE 7

The ball must be struck with the face of the mallet, the stroke being delivered whenever touching the ball it moves it. Should a stake or wire intervene the stroke is not allowed unless the ball is struck at the same time, and if the ball is moved, without being struck by the face of the mallet, it shall remain where it rests, and should a point or roquet be made, it shall not be allowed, except by the decision of the umpire as to the fairness of the shot. All balls thus moved by a false shot may be replaced or not at the option of the opponent, but no point or part of a point made shall be allowed.

RULE 8

A ball roquets, or counts upon, another upon which it has a right to play when it comes in contact with it by a blow from the player's mallet, or rebounds from a wicket or a stake, also when it comes in contact with it when play is taken from another ball.

RULE 9

When one ball thus roquets, or counts upon, another play *must be taken from it*. That ball is now dead. (See Rule 31.) After taking play from a ball and moving it, the player is entitled to one more stroke.

RULE 10

If a player in taking a Croquet from a ball, fails to move or shake it perceptibly such stroke ends his play, and his ball must be returned, or left where it stops, at the option of the opponent. He is not allowed to put his foot on playing ball.

RULE 11

When making a direct shot (i.e., roquet), the player must not push or follow the ball with his mallet; but when taking Croquet from a ball (two balls being in contact), he may follow his ball with the mallet; but must not strike it twice, give it a second impetus, or change the direction of the stroke.

RULE 12

If a player strikes his ball before his opponent has finished his play, the stroke shall stand, or be made over, at the option of the opponent. (See also Rule 58.)

RULE 13

A player may lightly tap any ball on the top to jar the sand off, or to make it stay where it belongs, or may have any adhering substance removed before making his stroke.

DIRECTION THROUGH WICKETS

RULE 14

In making all side or corner wickets the playing ball shall pass through them *towards* the center, not *away* from it.

RULE 15

Should a ball rest against or near a wire, and the umpire, or other person agreed on, should decide that in order to pass through the arch, an unfair or push shot would have to be made, it shall not be allowed if made.

(a) If a ball is in position or near any arch and the *arch* is hit by any ball in proper movements of play, and the ball is displaced the displacing of such ball and of any other balls must be accepted and any point or points made must stand.

FOUL STROKE

RULE 16

Should a player in making a stroke move with his mallet or mallet hand any other than his object ball, it shall be a foul and his play ceases, and all balls moved shall be replaced as before the stroke, or remain where they rest, at the option of the opponent.

RULE 17

If a dead ball (see Rule 31) in contact with another ball, moves on account of the inequality of the ground while playing the other ball *away from it,* the player does not lose his shot.

(a) If a live ball is similarly situated and moves on account of the inequality of the ground when the ball in contact is played away from it, the playing ball shall not be regarded as having counted upon it.

(b) If a ball, in proper course of play, rest against another ball, and in picking up the playing ball for the purpose of continuing the play, the other ball moves on account of the inequality of the ground, no attempt shall be made to replace it. [Note p. 63.]

RULE 18

A ball must not be touched while on the field, except when it is necessary to place it beside the ball that has been hit for the purpose of playing from it, or to replace it when it has been moved by accident — except by permission of the opponent. [Picking up wrong ball, therefore (Rule 62), ends play.] (See also Rule 13.)

RULE 19

A player after making roquet shall not stop his ball for the purpose of preventing its hitting another. Should he do so his play ceases and all balls shall be replaced as before the stroke, or remain, at the option of the opponent.

RULE 19

A player, in each turn of play, is at liberty to roquet any on the ground once only before making a point.

RULE 20

Should a player Croquet a ball he has not roqueted, he loses his turn, and all balls moved by such play must be replaced to the satisfaction of the umpire, or adversary. Should the mistake not be discovered before the player has made another stroke, the play shall be valid, and the player continue his play.

RULE 21

In taking Croquet from a ball, if player's ball strikes another, to which he is dead (see Rule 31), such stroke does not end his play, because it is not a direct shot. He is allowed to continue playing from the place where it stops.

RULE 22

If a player roquets two or more balls at the same stroke, only the first can be Croqueted, or used.

MARKING OF POINTS

RULE 23

A point is an arch or a stake. Therefore a player makes a point in the game when his ball makes an arch or hits a stake in proper play. (For *Rovers,* see Rule 57.)

RULE 24

If a player makes a point, and afterwards at the same stroke roquets a ball, he must take the point and use the ball, unless he is dead to such ball (see Rule 45), and such ball is beyond the *playing line*. In that case his play ceases. (See note to Rule 24, p. 63.)

RULE 25

Should the playing ball in making an arch roquet another that lies just through the arch, even if a dead ball, and then pass through it, the arch counts as well as the roquet. (See note to Rule 25; see also Rule 33.)

(*a*) If any ball not dead be resting under an arch and not through it, and the playing ball being for that arch strike it and then pass through, the arch is not allowed but the roquet counts.

RULE 26

If a ball roquets or counts upon another, and afterwards at the same stroke makes a point, it must take the ball and reject the point.

RULE 27

A player continues to play so long as he makes a point in the game, or roquets another ball to which he is in play.

RULE 28

A ball making two or more points at the same stroke, has only the same privilege as if it made but one.

RULE 29

Should a ball be driven through its arch, even by adversary or against the turning stake by any carom, combination, Croquet, or concussion by a stroke

16

not foul, it is a point made by that ball, and clip should be changed. (See Rule 5; for *Rovers* see Rule 57.)

JUMP SHOTS

RULE 30

Jump shots, on account of harm to the lawn, may be forbidden by local ground rules, or by mutual arrangement of players.

PLAYING ON DEAD BALL

RULE 31

A dead ball is one on which a player has no rights or one he has taken Croquet from in that turn of play.

RULE 32

If a player play by direct shot on a dead ball his play ceases and all balls displaced by such shot shall either be replaced in their former position, and the player's ball placed against the dead ball on the side from which it came, or, all balls shall rest where they He, at the option of the opponent. If driven off the field they must be properly placed. (See Rule 25; also latter part of Rule 24.)

RULE 33

Any point or part of a point or ball struck, after striking a dead ball is not allowed. It is a foul stroke. (See latter part of Rule 24; also Rule 25.)

RULE 34

A player may drive another ball by roquet or Croquet, or his own ball by Croquet, against a dead ball and give it a point or position, or displace it, and the dead ball shall not be replaced, nor shall any other ball moved by the stroke be replaced.

BALLS MOVED OR INTERFERED WITH BY ACCIDENT OR DESIGN

RULE 35

A ball accidentally displaced, otherwise than as provided for in Rule 16, must be returned to its position before play can proceed.

RULE 36

If a ball is stopped or diverted from its course by an opponent, the player may repeat the shot or not as he chooses. Should he decline to repeat the shot, the ball must remain where it ;tops, and, if playing ball, must play from there.

RULE 37

If a ball is stopped or diverted from its course by a player or his partner, the opponent may demand a repetition of the shot if he chooses. Should he decline to do so, the ball must remain where it stops, and, if playing ball, must play from there.

RULE 38

If a ball is stopped or diverted from its course by any object inside the ground, not pertaining to the game or ground, other than provided for in Rules 36 and 37, the shot may be repeated, or allowed to remain, at the option of the player. If not repeated, the ball must remain where it stops, and, if playing ball, play from there.

BALLS IN CONTACT

RULE 39

Should a player, on commencing his play, find his ball in contact with another, he may hit his own as he likes, and then have subsequent privileges, the same as though the balls were separated an inch or more.

RULES CONCERNING BOUNDARY

RULE 40

The *boundary line* is a strong cotton or other line extending around the field. The *playing line* is a line (imaginary or otherwise) two and one-half feet inside the boundary. This may be marked or not by chalk or by a smaller cord wired closely to the ground^ to allow a free stroke with the mallet.

BALLS OVER BOUNDARY LINE

RULE 41

A ball shot beyond the playing line, or the boundary line, must be returned inside the playing line and in a direction at right angles to the side or end of court. It follows that a ball off the field at any point not on a right angle to the side of court or the end is placed on the corner. (See Rules 46, 47, 48.)

(For full illustration see after the rules section.)

RULE 42

A ball is in the field and properly placed when the whole ball is within the playing line.

RULE 43

No play is allowed from beyond the playing line, except when a ball is placed in contact with another for the purpose of Croquet.

RULE 44

If a player strikes his ball when over the playing line, he shall lose his stroke, and all balls (displaced by shot) shall be replaced or left where they stop at the option of the opponent.

RULE 45

If a player hit a ball beyond the playing line by a direct shot, his play ceases, and the roqueted ball is placed on the playing line from the point where it lay before being thus hit. The playing ball is brought in from its resting place to its proper place on the playing line. But if a ball off the field is hit from a *Croquet,* the hit shall not be allowed, the balls to be replaced properly in the field from where they rest, and the play shall not cease.

RULE 46

The first ball driven over the playing line and returnable at the corner must be placed at or within the corner of *playing* lines.

RULE 47

If a ball, having been struck over the playing line, is returnable at the corner, another ball being on, or first entitled to, the corner, it shall be placed on that side of the corner ball on which it went off.

RULE 48

If two balls, having been shot over the playing line, should apparently require the same position, they shall be placed on the line alongside of each other in the same order in which they were played off.

BALL WHEN THROUGH AN ARCH

RULE 49

A ball is through an arch when a straight edge, laid across the two wires on the side from which the ball came, does not touch the ball.

BALLS - WHEN IN POSITION

RULE 50

If a ball has been placed under an arch, for the purpose of Croquet, it is not in position to run that arch. (See note. Rule 50.)

RULE 51

If a ball be driven under its arch from the wrong direction, and rests there, so that a straight edge laid against the wires on the side of the arch from which it came, fails to touch it, it is in position to run that arch in the right direction. If the straight edge touch the ball it cannot make the arch at the next stroke.

RULE 52

If a ball shot through its arch in the right direction, not having come in contact with another ball, rolls back through or under that arch, so that a straight edge applied as in Rule 49 touches it, the point is not made, but the ball is in position if left there.

HITTING BALL WHILE MAKING WICKET

RULE 53

The cage wicket may be made in one, two or many turns, provided the ball stops within the limits of the cage, (See Explanation of Terms, and cut opposite p. 64.)

RULE 54

Any playing ball within, or under a wicket, becomes dead to advancement through the wicket from that position, if it comes in contact with any other ball by a direct shot. (See Rule 25; also note to Rule 54.)

ROVERS

RULE 55

A player becomes a rover when he has made all the points in regular order to the home stake.

RULE 56

A rover has the right of roquet and consequent Croquet on every other ball once during each turn of play, and is subject to roquet and Croquet by any ball in play, but an opponent cannot put a rover out.

RULE 57

Only a partner rover can put a rover out, and if one makes the other to hit the stake and then itself fails to hit, neither is out. A rover having been driven against the stake and over the boundary or playing line, must be properly placed to await the hitting of the stake by its partner. It cannot be moved from this proper placement to allow the partner ball to hit the stake. They must go out in successive strokes or both remain in play. (a) If a player become a rover by the stroke that causes a partner ball to become a rover, and possibly to hit the stake, the partner may be regarded as out, provided the player desires to try the stake on the next stroke. If not, he may make any proper plays necessary to finish the game, as he is now alive on all balls.

PLAYING OUT OF TURN. OR WRONG BALL

RULE 58

If a player plays out of his proper turn, or in his proper turn plays the wrong ball, and the mistake is discovered before the next player has commenced his play, all benefit from any point or points made is lost, and his turn of play is forfeited. All balls moved by the misplay must be returned to their former position by the umpire or adversary. But if the mistake is not discovered until after the next player has made his first stroke, the error must stand. (See Rule 12.)

POINTS RE-MADE

RULE 59

If a player makes a point he has already made in that turn and the mistake is discovered before the proper point is made, the play ceases, with the shot by which the point was re-made, and the marker is placed at its proper point. All balls shall be left in the position they had at the time the point was re-made. If not discovered before the proper point is made, the points so made are good, and play proceeds the same as if no error had been made. (See also Rule 5.)

ERROR IN ORDER OF PLAY

RULE 60

If an error in order is discovered after a player has struck his ball, he shall be allowed to finish his play, provided he is playing in the regular sequence of his partner's ball last played. In that case the error would belong to the previous player, but his play and any points made must stand. In case of dispute upon any point at any time, it shall be decided by the umpire; if there is no umpire, by lot. No recourse shall be had to lot unless each party expresses the belief that the other is wrong.

CHANGING SURFACE OF GROUND

RULE 61

A player, before or during his play, may require either arches or grounds or anything pertaining thereto to be placed in proper condition.

PENALTY-GENERAL RULE

RULE 62

If a rule is violated, a penalty for which has not been provided, the player shall cease his play.

Notes on Rules

Note to Rule 1 — A notice conspicuously posted comprising the substance of Rule 1 will be of much service to spectators in keeping them in line with the strictest proprieties. The players should receive no benefit or harm from the conversation of spectators, and no suggestion should ever be presented by any spectator.

Note to Rule 17. — It is evident that, if the court is perfect, *playing away from* another ball cannot possibly cause it to move. Hence the rule.

Note to Rule 17b. — Suppose a (playing) ball to be in contact with a ball that is through its arch as a straightedge would show. If playing ball be removed for further use, and the other ball comes back to a position that allows it to be touched by the straightedge from its playing side, such ball is *not through the arch.*

Note to Rule 24. — This latter part needs thought and attention. If a ball, though it passes through its arch, hits a ball beyond the *playing line* play ceases because of Rule 45.

Note to Rule 25. — While this is not mathematically correct, the rule is so made to avoid disputes and difficult measurements.

Note to Rule 50. — To place a ball *"under an arch"* (i.e., for the purpose of taking Croquet from another ball) means that if the arch should be pushed into the ground perfectly vertically the arch would touch a segment of the ball. If the ball could not be touched it would not be *under* the arch.

Note to Rule 54. — This rule was made especially for balls at the center wicket, but is also applicable at single wickets. To illustrate: The playing ball, in passing into the double center wicket through the first part of it, hits by *direct* shot another ball. The player cannot place his ball against it and pass on through the wicket by a Croquet, but must re-enter the wicket. If, however, the playing ball enters the first arch from a *Croquet,* or split shot, and hits and remains in contact with a live ball, if no space is gained by placing it, it can by roquet both go through itself and also put this other ball through.

CAGE LIMITS SHOWN.

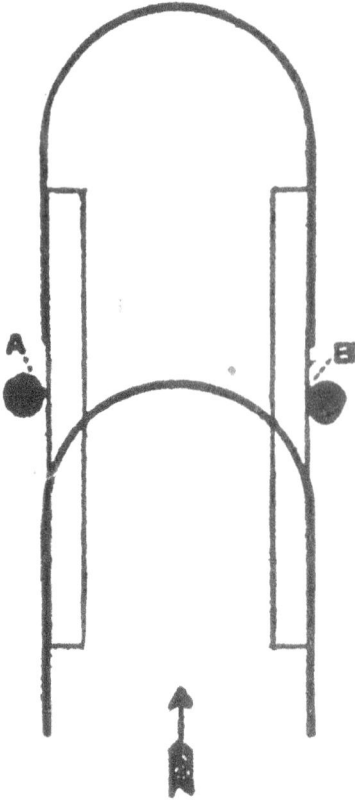

JUMP SHOT SHOWN.

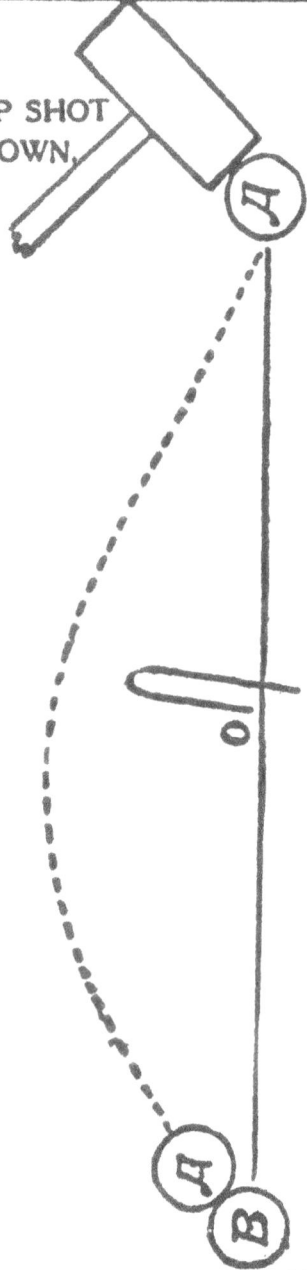

A — Straight-edge does <u>not</u> touch Ball. Ball is <u>without</u> the cage limits.

B — Straight-edge <u>touches</u> Ball. Ball is <u>within</u> the cage limits.

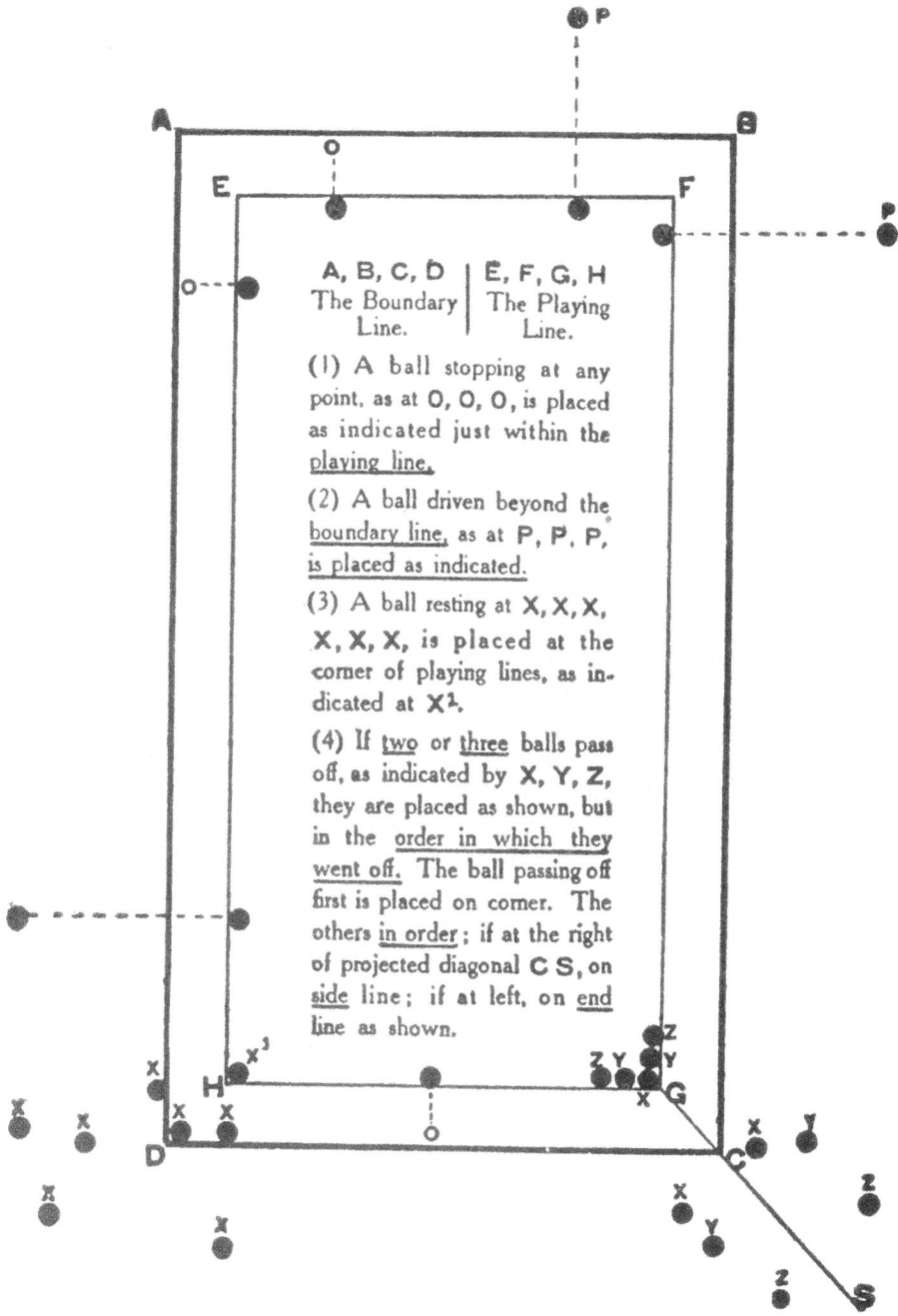

A, B, C, D	E, F, G, H
The Boundary Line.	The Playing Line.

(1) A ball stopping at any point, as at O, O, O, is placed as indicated just within the playing line.

(2) A ball driven beyond the boundary line, as at P, P, P, is placed as indicated.

(3) A ball resting at X, X, X, X, X, X, is placed at the corner of playing lines, as indicated at X^1.

(4) If two or three balls pass off, as indicated by X, Y, Z, they are placed as shown, but in the order in which they went off. The ball passing off first is placed on corner. The others in order; if at the right of projected diagonal C S, on side line; if at left, on end line as shown.

Official Laws - British Croquet Association

THE GAME

1. The game of Croquet is played between two sides, playing alternate "turns" (Law 23), each side consisting either of one or of two players. Four balls, coloured respectively Blue, Red, Black, and Yellow, are played in the sequence named, one side playing Blue and Black, and the other Red and Yellow. When a side consists of two players, one partner plays throughout with one ball of the side, and the other partner with the other. The game is won by the side which first makes all its "points" in order (Law 15) subject to Law 22a.

THE GROUND

2. The ground shall be rectangular, 35 yards in length by 28 yards in width, within a defined boundary, which alone shall of necessity be marked by a continuous line. A flag shall be placed at each corner. The sides of an inner rectangle, parallel to and distant 3 feet from the boundary, are called the "Yard-line," its corners the "Corner-spots," and the space between the Yard-line and the boundary the "Yard-line Area." Portions of the Yardline Area, 14 yards long, called Baulks A and B shall be defined as shown on the diagrams. A ball played from within a baulk may be placed on either of its inner boundaries, but must not overhang any of the boundary lines of the ground.

Eight white pegs, not exceeding ¾ of an inch in diameter or 3 inches in height above the ground, shall be placed on the boundary, at distances of 3 feet from the corners of the boundary. The square yard formed at each corner by the two corner pegs, the corner spot, and the corner flag is called a "Corner Square."

HOOPS AND PEGS

3. The hoops shall be of round iron, from 5/8 to ¾ inch in diameter, and of uniform thickness. They shall be 12 inches in height above the ground, vertical, and firmly fixed.

The crown shall be straight, and at right angles to the uprights which shall be from 3¾ to 4 inches apart (inside measurement) from the ground upwards.

The turning peg and the winning peg shall be of wood, of a uniform diameter above the ground of 1½ inches. They shall be 18 inches in height above the ground, vertical, and firmly fixed.

No hoop or peg may be adjusted except by the umpire, or with the consent of the adversary.

SETTINGS

4. The setting of the hoops and pegs shall be in accordance with one of the diagrams following, the order of making the "points" being indicated by the arrows.

In both settings each corner hoop is 7 yards from the two adjacent boundaries. In Setting No. 1 the two pegs and the two central hoops are placed along the central line of the ground at intervals of 7 yards. In setting No. 2 the turning peg is omitted, the winning peg is equidistant from the four corners, and the two central hoops are placed on the central line, 7 yards on each side of the winning peg.

MALLETS

5. The head of the mallet shall be of wood only, except that metal may be used for weighting or strengthening it. The two end faces shall be parallel, of wood only, and identical in every respect. A player may not change his mallet more than once during a game, except in the case of bona fide damage.

BALLS

6. The ball shall be 3 5/8 inches in diameter, and of even weight, which shall be not less than 15¾ oz. nor more than 16¼ oz.

CLIPS

7. The hoop or peg next in order for every ball at the commencement of a turn shall be distinguished by a clip of a colour corresponding with that of the ball. The clip shall be placed on the crown of the hoop until six hoops have been run by the corresponding ball, and afterwards on one of the uprights.

THE STRIKER

8. The player whose turn it is to play, or who has made any stroke called in question, is called the "Striker," and the ball with which he is or has been playing any particular turn is called the "striker's ball." Apart from the actual making of the stroke, the striker's partner has the same privileges (except as provided by Law 19) and is subject to the same penalties as the striker. If the players' cannot come to an agreement on any question of fact, the striker's opinion shall prevail, except as provided by Law 35.

TAKING AIM AND THE STROKE

9. The striker shall be deemed to be "taking aim" when he has begun to put himself in position to strike a ball. A "stroke" is deemed to have been made if

the striker "move" a ball with his mallet in taking aim, or if he make a forward or downward movement of his mallet with intent to strike a ball. A ball is deemed to have been moved if it leave its position and remain in another. A stroke is concluded as soon as all balls set in motion by it have either come to rest or reached the boundary.

MARKING DIRECTION OF AIM

10. No mark shall be made upon the ground, either within or without the boundary, for the purpose of guiding the striker in the direction or strength of a stroke; anything placed or held for this purpose must be removed to the satisfaction of the adversary before the strike is made. A breach of this law gives the adversary the option of having the stroke made again.

CHOICE OF LEAD AND OF BALLS

11. The winner of the toss shall decide whether he will take the choice of lead or the choice of balls. If he take the choice of lead the adversary has the choice of balls, and vice versa. When a match consists of more than one game the privilege of deciding shall follow alternately. The side playing first may commence with either ball of the side.

THE COMMENCEMENT OF THE GAME

12. The first "turn" of each ball shall commence from Baulk "A." As soon as a stroke has been made with a ball it is "in play," and continues to be in play, except when "in hand" (Law 17) or "off the ground" (Law 26), until it has made all its points in order.

BALL IN POSITION FOR HOOP

13. A ball is "in position" for running its hoop either (1) If, whether in hand or not, it lie on the "playing side" of the hoop, or (2) If it has previously entered the hoop from the "playing side" and has not subsequently been clear of it or become "in hand." The "playing side" of the hoop is the side from which the ball has to run that hoop in order.

A ball is deemed to be lying on one side of a hoop when it cannot be touched by a straight edge placed against the uprights on the other side.

HOOP, WHEN RUN

14. A ball has "run" its hoop when, starting from position for that hoop, it has passed through, and finally come to rest on the non-playing side.

In all cases the question must be decided without any adjustment of the hoop; should any player touch the hoop before the question is decided, the other side has the option whether the point shall be scored or not.

A POINT

15. When a ball in play runs a hoop in order, or hits a peg in order, it is said to make a "point." The striker may make points for any ball (subject to Law 22), and may make any number of points in a single stroke. Whenever the striker makes a point for his own ball he shall make another stroke (subject to Law 20), unless that point be the winning peg.

If, at the commencement of a turn, the striker find his ball lying in contact with a peg in order, he may, at his option, either score the point without making a stroke, or play his ball in a direction away from the peg, in which case the point is not scored. A ball other than the striker's, lying in contact with a peg in order, cannot score the point.

PLACING OF CLIPS

16. In the absence of an umpire the striker is responsible, at the conclusion of his turn, for the correct placing of any clips which have been or should have been moved during that turn. Should he fail to place any clip correctly, and the adversary in consequence make any stroke or strokes under a misapprehension, he shall be entitled to make again any such stroke or strokes, provided that he claim to do so before the commencement of the subsequent turn.

Should the players be unable to agree as to the correct position of any clip, its actual position at the time shall be taken as correct.

ROQUET AND BALL IN HAND

17. The striker makes a "roquet" when his ball in play hits another ball in play, provided that since he last "took croquet" from that ball, he has either made a point for his ball or commenced a fresh turn. On making a roquet the striker's ball immediately becomes "in hand," and remains so until "croquet" is taken (subject to Law 20). A ball displaced during a stroke by a ball in hand shall not be replaced, and any point made for a ball so displaced shall be scored. Should a ball in hand be touched by an adversary before the stroke is concluded, the striker may make the stroke again.

BALLS ROQUETED SIMULTANEOUSLY, ETC.

18. If the striker roquet two or more balls simultaneously he may "take croquet" from whichever he chooses; he may not take croquet from any other such ball until he has roqueted it again. If the striker roquet a ball and hit a

peg in order simultaneously, he may choose whether he will take croquet or score the point.

TAKING CROQUET

19. The striker, when he has roqueted a ball, shall "take croquet" by placing his ball, or causing it to be placed by his partner, in contact with the ball roqueted (see Law 30), and with that ball only, and then making a stroke. In making the stroke he must move or shake perceptibly the croqueted ball, or a ball in contact with it other than the striker's ball. Should he fail to do so the turn ceases, the balls shall remain where they lie, and any points made by such stroke shall not be scored. Should the striker, if challenged, be unable to assert definitely that he himself saw the required movement, the croqueted ball shall be deemed not to have been perceptibly moved or shaken. The striker shall not place his foot on either ball while making the stroke. If, before the stroke is concluded, the striker's ball again hit the croqueted ball, a roquet is deemed not to have been made, even though the striker's ball has made a point. After taking croquet the striker shall make another stroke (subject to Laws 20 and 22).

CROQUET-STROKE AND BOUNDARY

20. When the striker takes croquet: — (1) If the striker's ball be sent off the ground (Law 26) without making a roquet the turn shall cease; (2) If the croqueted ball be sent off the ground the turn shall cease, and in this case, if a roquet be made by the striker's ball, both it and the ball roqueted shall remain where they lie (subject to Laws 26 and 29).

In either case any points made (see Law 15) shall be scored.

HOOP AND ROQUET IN SAME STROKE

21. If the striker's ball, being in position for running its hoop, pass between the uprights, and in the same stroke, while still in play, hit a ball lying on the non-playing side, finally coming to rest on that side, the hoop is run and a roquet made. But unless the ball hit be lying on the non-playing side, the hoop is not scored if a roquet be made.

ROVER AND PEGGING OUT

22. A ball which has made all its points in order except the winning peg is called a "rover."

When a rover scores the winning peg in order, it is said to be "pegged out."

The striker must remove from the ground a ball pegged out. Should he continue his turn without doing so, the adversary may require him to make again the stroke immediately following the omission.

The striker cannot peg out a ball, other than his own, unless his ball be a rover at the commencement of the stroke. Should the striker peg out a rover by roqueting it, his turn shall at once cease.

A ball in play displaced by a ball pegged out shall remain where it comes to rest (subject to Laws 26 and 29), Any point made for a ball so displaced shall be scored.

TIME LIMIT AFTER PEGGING OUT

22a. — When one or more balls have been pegged out the game shall be deemed to be finished at the expiration of one hour from the time at which the first ball was pegged out, whether the turn is concluded or not, but the striker may first play a stroke for which he has already begun to take aim when time is called, and any point made by such stroke shall be scored. The side which has then scored the most points shall win. If the points are equal when time is so called, the side which, at the completion of that or a subsequent turn, has scored the most points, shall win.

THE TURN

23. A "turn" consists of a concluded stroke or a succession of such strokes. A turn begins when the striker has begun to take aim for the first stroke of that turn, or has moved a ball with the intention of commencing a turn. In every turn the striker may roquet each ball before .making a point, and may do so again after each point made for his own ball.

Whenever the striker scores a point for his own ball, or makes a roquet, or takes croquet, he shall continue his turn (subject to Laws 20 and 22).

All strokes made after the conclusion of a turn by the player of that turn (except with the evident intention of playing a bisque), and all strokes made at any time by a player playing instead of an adversary, are null and void. Any balls displaced by such strokes shall be replaced.

Should the striker, at the commencement of his turn, be in doubt as to which ball he ought to play, he is entitled to be informed by the adversary. If misinformed he may, at any time before the adversary plays, recommence the turn.

BALL LYING IN A HOLE

24. A ball lying in a hole, other than one on a corner spot, must not be moved without the sanction of a Referee. The striker may move a ball lying in a hole on a corner spot provided that it be his own ball or in contact with his own ball. When moving such ball the striker may place it just clear of the hole, in the line of aim.

WIRING

25. The striker's ball is said to be "wired" from another ball if (1) Any part of a peg or an upright would impede the direct course of any part of it towards any part of the other ball; or (2) Any part of a peg or hoop so interferes with any part of the swing of the mallet that the striker cannot drive his ball freely towards any part of the other ball. The mere interference of a hoop or peg with the stance of the striker does not constitute wiring.

If at the commencement of a turn, by the decision of an umpire or the admission of the adversary, the striker's ball be wired from all the other balls, the striker, provided that it was placed in its present position by the stroke of an adversary, may lift it and play it from that baulk which he, the striker, may select.

BALL OFF THE GROUND

26. A ball is said to be "off the ground" when any part of it, at the conclusion of or during a stroke, touches or overhangs the boundary, or touches a corner peg or flag. When a ball in play is sent off the ground the striker shall at once place it on the yard-line directly opposite to the point on the boundary first reached by it (except as provided by Law 27). All balls so placed are called "yard-line balls," and any ball in contact with a yard-line ball becomes itself a yard-line ball. If any other ball or balls already on or near the yard-line interfere with the correct placing of a ball sent off the ground, the striker shall place the ball sent off on the yard-line, in contact with any one of such balls, and they and the ball so placed shall be deemed to be in contact with one another.

CORNER BALLS

27. When a ball in play is sent off the ground within 3 feet of a corner, or comes to rest within a corner square, the striker shall at once place it on the corner spot (except as provided by Law 29.) If it cannot be so placed the striker shall place it on the yard-line, as near as possible to the corner spot. All balls so placed are called "corner balls," and any ball in contact with a corner ball becomes itself a corner ball, and all corner balls at one corner shall be deemed to be in contact with one another. In cases of doubt under Law 26 a ball which has touched a corner peg shall be treated as a corner ball.

BALLS IN CONTACT

28, If the strikers ball in play be in contact with one or more balls, a roquet (counting as a stroke) shall be deemed to have been made, and the striker shall take croquet from one of such balls at his option.

If the striker's ball be one of two or more corner or yard-line balls in contact, the striker may take croquet from any one of such balls at his option. Before doing so he may place all such balls in any position, provided that, in the case of corner balls, one be placed on the corner spot, and in the case of yard-line balls, one be placed on the spot which one of them originally occupied; and provided also that every such ball be placed in contact with one of the others, all being in contact.

Setting No. 1

Scale 1 : 360, or one-tenth of an inch to a yard.

33

Setting No. 2

Scale 1:360, or one-tenth of an inch to a yard.

In all cases the striker shall take croquet off any ball which he may have actually roqueted.

34

BALL IN YARD-LINE AREA

29. A ball in play in the yard-line area shall at once be placed on the nearest point of the yard-line, as in Law 26, and becomes a yard-line ball. But if such ball be the striker's ball during a turn, the striker shall play it from where it lies.

BALL NOT CORRECTLY PLACED

30. If the striker make a stroke while any ball (including his own ball), which might have either obstructed the striker or been moved by the stroke, is not correctly placed, the adversary, unless such ball was incorrectly placed by himself, may require the balls to be correctly placed and the stroke to be made again.

BOUNDARY, ETC., INTERFERING WITH STROKE

31. If the striker find that the height of the boundary, or of any fixed obstacle outside it, is likely to interfere with his stroke, he may, to the satisfaction of the adversary, move his ball, and any other ball likely to be affected by the stroke, sufficiently to allow a free swing of the mallet. In so doing he must move his own ball along the line of aim, and the relative positions of any other balls so moved must be maintained. Any ball so moved, and not displaced by the stroke, shall at once be replaced.

BALL DISPLACED

32. (a) Should a ball at rest be moved accidently by the striker (except in striking or in taking aim), or by an adversary, it shall be replaced without penalty.

(b) Should a ball in play, when moving, be touched by an adversary, the striker shall elect whether he will make the stroke again, or whether the ball shall remain where it came to rest, or be placed where in his judgment it would, but for such interference, have finally come to rest; but no point or roquet not actually made shall be claimed as the result of such stroke.

(c) Should a ball at rest be removed by any agency outside the match, it shall be replaced.

(d) Should a ball in play, when moving, be interfered with by any agency outside the match, the striker may make the stroke again.

(e) Should a ball at rest make a point not due to the action of the striker, the ball shall be replaced and the point shall not be scored.

PLAYING WITH A WRONG BALL, OR OUT OF TURN

33. If before the four balls are in play the first stroke of any turn be played with a ball in wrong sequence, such stroke and all subsequent strokes in any

turn are null and void, provided that the error be announced before the fifth turn of the game is commenced. In all other cases, if the striker play with a wrong ball, or if a player play instead of his partner, he shall be adjudged to have made a foul (Law 34), provided that the error be announced before the commencement of another ordinary turn. Should more than one stroke have been played with a wrong ball, or out of turn, before the error is announced, the balls shall be replaced as they were after the first stroke in error was made, and the adversary shall then exact the penalty for a foul.

If the players be unable to agree as to the position the balls were in after the first stroke in error was made, the striker's opinion shall prevail (Law 8).

On the error being announced after another ordinary turn has been commenced, all points made during the erroneous turn shall be scored, except points made for any ball by an adversary's ball wrongly played with; and unless the player commencing the next ordinary turn has continued the sequence of balls and players which would have been in order if the error in the previous turn had not occurred, he shall be adjudged to have played with a wrong ball, or out of turn, and in this case the balls shall be replaced and the turn recommenced without penalty.

FOULS

34. If the striker make a foul his turn shall at once cease, and any point made during the stroke in which the foul occurred shall not be scored. Balls moved by such stroke shall either remain where they come to rest or be replaced, at the option of the adversary. A foul cannot be claimed after a fresh ordinary turn has been commenced.

In addition to the cases provided for by Law 33 the striker makes a foul if he —

(a) Hit his ball with any part of the mallet other than an end face of the head, in making a stroke; or hold the mallet otherwise than by the shaft only; or cause or attempt to cause the mallet to hit the ball by kicking or striking the mallet.

(b) Touch with the mallet or unlawfully move a ball other than his own ball, in taking aim or in striking.

(c) Push or pull his ball, when taking croquet, without first striking it audibly or distinctly,

(d) Push or pull his ball, when not taking croquet, whether he first strike it audibly or not.

(e) Strike his ball twice in the same stroke, unless such ball be in hand.

(f) Take croquet from two balls simultaneously.

(g) Touch a ball when in play and moving except with his own ball in hand when in the act of striking.

(h) Allow a ball when in play and moving to touch him, or his mallet, or his clothes, except a rover rebounding from the winning peg when pegged out.

(k) Move his ball, when making a stroke, by striking a peg or a hoop without striking the ball.

(l) Make a stroke after a roquet without taking croquet.

(m) Strike his ball so as to cause it to touch a peg, or an upright of a hoop, while still in contact with the mallet, and while still in play.

(n) Strike his ball, when lying in contact with a peg, or an upright of a hoop, otherwise than away from that peg or upright.

(o) Move a ball in play intentionally in a manner not provided for by the Laws. In this case the ball or balls moved must be replaced.

BISQUES

35. A "bisque" is an extra turn (see Law 23) given in a game played under handicap. A "half-bisque" is a restricted bisque in which no point can be scored for any ball. The giver of odds shall keep a record of the bisques played. In the event of any dispute his decision on this point shall, in the absence of an Umpire, be final.

(a) The striker may play a bisque or half-bisque to which he may be entitled, either immediately after concluding his ordinary turn, and with the same ball, or immediately after concluding a bisque in which he has not made a roquet or scored a point for his ball; but he may not play a bisque immediately after a half-bisque.

If the striker was entitled to play either a bisque or a half-bisque, he shall be adjudged to have played the bisque, unless before commencing the extra turn he has announced his intention of playing the half-bisque.

(b) If the striker, at the conclusion of his turn, definitely announce in reply to an adversary that he does not intend to play a bisque, his option of playing it thereby ceases.

(c) If the striker, before the conclusion of his ordinary turn, purport to play a bisque, he shall be adjudged not to have played it, the balls shall be replaced without penalty, and the ordinary turn shall be continued.

(d) If the striker, after concluding a turn with the right ball, make a stroke of a bisque with a wrong ball, the bisque shall be adjudged to have been played, and the penalty under Law 33 shall be exacted on the bisque turn.

(e) If the striker, after concluding an ordinary turn with a wrong ball without the error being announced, commence a bisque with that ball or the right ball, the bisque shall be adjudged not to have been played, and the penalty under Law 23 shall be exacted on the ordinary turn just concluded.

(f) The adversary, by forfeiting 3 bisques, may at any time after the first stroke of the striker's turn declare such turn to be at an end; such declaration shall be made before the striker has commenced to take aim, but after a roquet has been made forfeiture cannot be declared until croquet has been taken.

UMPIRES

36. Either side may claim that an Umpire, agreed on by the two sides, be appointed for any part of a game. The Umpire's opinion on all questions of fact or replacement shall in all cases override the striker's. The duties of an Umpire are: —

(a) To draw attention to any breach of the Laws, deciding, whether appealed to or not, all questions of fact.

(b) To move the clips, or to see that they are properly moved.

(c) To adjust hoops and pegs in accordance with Law 3.

ERRORS NOT PROVIDED FOR

37. Except as provided in these Laws, no errors or omissions can be claimed after the next ordinary turn has commenced, or after the game has been concluded, or after all the players have left the ground in the belief that the game has been concluded.

Alternative Laws

When the game is played under the following "Alternative Laws," or either of them, the preceding Laws shall be interpreted accordingly.

PLAYING WITH EITHER BALL OF THE SIDE

A. The Game of Croquet is played between two sides, playing alternate '"turns" (Law 23), each side consisting either of one or of two players. Four balls, coloured respectively Blue, Red, Black and Yellow, are played in the sequence named, one side playing Blue and Black and the other Red and Yellow. *After they are all in play any ordinary turn may be played by either ball of the side.* When a side consists of two players, one partner plays throughout with one ball of the side, and the other partner with the other. The game is won by the side which first makes all its "points" in order (Law 15 and Law 22a').

Law 25 is applicable to both balls of a side.

DOUBLE DEAD BOUNDARY

B. After the first stroke of a turn, if any ball, except a ball in hand, or a yard-line or corner ball, be sent' off the ground (Law 26), the turn shall at once cease, but this Law shall not apply to the striker of the partner ball of a ball pegged out.

COPY REGULATION

The Committee of any Tournament shall have the power to notify in their programme that all or any of the Events shall be played under both or either of the "Alternative Laws" A. and B.

APPROXIMATE SCALE

In a game commencing at the	2nd Hoop. $\left(\frac{18}{20}\right)$	3rd Hoop. $\left(\frac{16}{20}\right)$	4th Hoop. $\left(\frac{14}{20}\right)$	5th Hoop. $\left(\frac{13}{20}\right)$	6th Hoop. $\left(\frac{12}{20}\right)$	7th Hoop. $\left(\frac{11}{20}\right)$
A difference in Handicap of a ¼ bisque becomes	0	0	0	0	0	0
,, ,, ½ bisque ,,	½	½	½	½	½	½
,, ,, ¾ of a bisque ,,	½	½	½	½	½	½
,, ,, 1 bisque ,,	1	1	½	½	½	½
,, ,, 1¼ bisques ,,	1	1	1	1	1	½
,, ,, 1½ ,, ,,	1½	1	1	1	1	1
,, ,, 1¾ ,, ,,	1½	1½	1	1	1	1
,, ,, 2 ,, ,,	2	1½	1½	1½	1	1
,, ,, 2¼ ,, ,,	2	2	1½	1½	1½	1
,, ,, 2½ ,, ,,	2½	2	2	1½	1½	1½
,, ,, 2¾ ,, ,,	2½	2	2	2	1½	1½
,, ,, 3 ,, ,,	2½	2½	2	2	2	1½
,, ,, 3¼ ,, ,,	3	2½	2½	2	2	2
,, ,, 3½ ,, ,,	3	3	2½	2½	2	2
,, ,, 3¾ ,, ,,	3½	3	2½	2½	2½	2
,, ,, 4 ,, ,,	3½	3	3	2½	2½	2
,, ,, 4¼ ,, ,,	4	3½	3	3	2½	2½
,, ,, 4½ ,, ,,	4	3½	3	3	2½	2½
,, ,, 4¾ ,, ,,	4½	4	3½	3	3	2½
,, ,, 5 ,, ,,	4½	4	3½	3½	3	3
,, ,, 5¼ ,, ,,	4½	4	3½	3½	3	3
,, ,, 5½ ,, ,,	5	4½	4	3½	3½	3
,, ,, 5¾ ,, ,,	5	4½	4	3½	3½	3
,, ,, 6 ,, ,,	5½	5	4	4	3½	3½
,, ,, 6¼ ,, ,,	5½	5	4½	4	4	3½
,, ,, 6½ ,, ,,	6	5	4½	4	4	3½
,, ,, 6¾ ,, ,,	6	5½	4½	4½	4	3½
,, ,, 7 ,, ,,	6½	5½	5	4½	4	4
,, ,, 7¼ ,, ,,	6½	6	5	4½	4½	4
,, ,, 7½ ,, ,,	7	6	5½	5	4½	4
,, ,, 7¾ ,, ,,	7	6	5½	5	4½	4½
,, ,, 8 ,, ,,	7	6½	5½	5	5	4½
,, ,, 8¼ ,, ,,	7½	6½	6	5½	5	4½
,, ,, 8½ ,, ,,	7½	7	6	5½	5	4½
,, ,, 8¾ ,, ,,	8	7	6	5½	5½	5
,, ,, 9 ,, ,,	8	7	6½	6	5½	5
,, ,, 9¼ ,, ,,	8½	7½	6½	6	5½	5
,, ,, 9½ ,, ,,	8½	7½	6½	6	5½	5
,, ,, 9¾ ,, ,,	9	8	7	6½	6	5½
,, ,, 10 ,, ,,	9	8	7	6½	6	5½
,, ,, 10¼ ,, ,,	9	8	7	6½	6	5½
,, ,, 10½ ,, ,,	9½	8½	7½	7	6½	6
,, ,, 10¾ ,, ,,	9½	8½	7½	7	6½	6
,, ,, 11 ,, ,,	10	9	7½	7	6½	6
,, ,, 11¼ ,, ,,	10	9	8	7½	7	6
,, ,, 11½ ,, ,,	10½	9	8	7½	7	6½
,, ,, 11¾ ,, ,,	10½	9½	8	7½	7	6½
,, ,, 12 ,, ,,	11	9½	8½	8	7	6½
,, ,, 12¼ ,, ,,	11	10	8½	8	7½	6½
,, ,, 12½ ,, ,,	11½	10	9	8	7½	7

www.ingramcontent.com/pod-product-compliance
Lightning Source LLC
Chambersburg PA
CBHW021921040426
42448CB00007B/861